SCO HOROSCOPE

2017

Lisa Lazuli

Lisa Lazuli is the author of the amazon bestseller:

HOROSCOPE 2014: Astrology and Numerology Horoscopes

As well as:

HOROSCOPE 2015: Astrology and Numerology Horoscopes

HOROSCOPE 2016: Astrology and Numerology Horoscopes

Those who enjoy astrology many also enjoy my book on Numerology:

Numerology Deciphered

Or my You Tube Channel

Lisa Lazuli Astrology

Cover Art: Gorbash Varvara on Shutterstock

ABOUT THE AUTHOR

Lisa Lazuli studied astrology with the Faculty of Astrological Studies in London.

She has practiced since 1999.

Lisa has been a regular guest on BBWM and BBC Shropshire talking about astrology and doing both horoscopes and live readings. She has also made guest appearances on Fox FM, BBC Cambridgeshire, BBC Northamptonshire, BBC Coventry and Warwickshire and US Internet Radio Shows including the Debra Clement Show.

Lisa wrote horoscopes for Asian Woman Magazine.

Lisa's Brexit prediction vlog on youtube was extremely well received and Lisa also successfully predicted that Teresa May would become the next UK Prime Minister and that Donald Trump would win the US election. Lisa continues to add to her youtube channel with political predictions and relationship astrology.

Now available:

TAURUS: Your Day, Your Decan, Your Sign

The most REVEALING book on The Bull yet.

and

GEMINI: Your Day, Your Decan, Your Sign

A stunning insight into the Twins

Lisa Lazuli is also the author of

The mystery/thrillers:

A Sealed Fate – Now in AUDIO BOOK

Holly Leaves

Next of Sin

As well as:

ARIES HOROSCOPE 2017

TAURUS HOROSCOPE 2017

GEMINI HOROSCOPE 2017

CANCER HOROSCOPE 2017

LEO HOROSCOPE 2017

VIRGO HOROSCOPE 2017

LIBRA HOROSCOPE 2017

Also in kindle and paperback:

Delicious, Nutritious Recipes for the Time and Cash Strapped

Paleo Diet: Get Started, Get Motivated, Feel Great.

99 ACE Places to Promote Your Book

Pressure Cooking Reinvented.

Sugar Free Desserts with Pazaz

Sugar-Free Cakes, Cookies, Muffins and Tarts: Sugar-Free Cakes, Cookies, Muffins and Tarts

Depression Busters – The diet to get you on the road to better mental health

Alternative Medicine for Pets: Your Guide to Holistic Health for your Dog and Cat

Wheat and Gluten-Free Bread, Rolls, and Biscuits: 50 Exciting Recipes using Healthful and Inspiring Ingredients WHEAT FREE

THE VEGETARIAN ROUTE TO WEIGHT LOSS: OVER 50 DELICIOUS RECIPES

FOREWARD

Dear Reader,

I hope my yearly horoscope for Libra will provide you with some insightful guidance during what is a very tricky time astrologically speaking, with the heavy planets i.e. Pluto and Uranus at loggerheads in cardinal signs, and Neptune in Pisces calling us all to get in touch with our spiritual side.

I have a conversational style of writing, please excuse any grammatical errors, I write much as I would speak.

As the song goes, "Nobody said it was easy". I know the mass media pump out shows aplenty about quick fix love, money, fame and success; however, life is a journey filled with challenges and obstacles designed to encourage us to find out what we are made of and who we really are.

Embrace the good and bad and enjoy what your unique experience is.

Be the hero in your own personal life movie and never hide your spotlight.

I must add that the best astrology insights are gained from a unique chart based on your time, date, year and place of birth.

Please join me on Facebook:

https://www.facebook.com/pages/Lisa-Lazuli-Astrologer/192000594298158?ref=hl

Contents

OVERVIEW

This year is ideal for pursuing goals of which you are the heart. 2017 is about developing your ideas, becoming clearer about your motivations and getting more resolved in your stance. It is a good year to make important decisions; especially ones where you have to deal with much information. This is a good year for dealing with bureaucracy: you can deal with the forms relating to setting up a business, immigration, applying for funds or jobs. You can take on a great deal of information or facts this year, and so it is perfect for remembering lines, giving presentation or writing papers. Words, not deeds is very much the phrase that is pertinent this year as you can have a great deal of impact with the power of what you put out regarding information or views put across in the medium of prose, fiction, lyrics, or poetry.

You are very passionate and staunch in your views and can be very persuasive if not downright dogmatic; however, your passion and unswerving belief can inspire and motivate others. Scorpio can be the voice that gives other voices the courage to come forward.

This is a productive and busy year that is both varied, exciting, and nerve wracking. There may not be radical change, but there can be loads of little changes which add up to an exciting and dynamic year. This is a great time to begin new projects, hobbies or set goals – the most successful goals will be those related to learning, distributing information, trading, starting new business contracts, writing and speaking. You have a clear vision and are single-minded. This is a very powerful time as you have conviction and will nail your colours to the mast, going your own way and sticking to your guns.

This is an exceptional time for using the law of attraction: positive thoughts and internal attitudes become positive realities which bring your confidence levels up and further inspire you. As you see things in your life taking shape and moving forward, you will become happier and more content, and this aids all your relationships and also your sense of inner ease. Scorpio are a sign that suffer emotionally in that you are often turbulent and fiery emotions play havoc with your nerves or digestive health; however, this year a great amount of inner peace aids general health and vitality, which is great news.

2017 is a year when you accept challenges with a greater level of detachment; you will not let them get you down or change your mindset; you will greet them with vigour and a spirit that says, you will win and prevail.

This is a wonderful quote for Scorpio this year:

"If you can dream—and not make dreams your master;
If you can think—and not make thoughts your aim;
If you can meet with Triumph and Disaster
And treat those two impostors just the same" Rudyard Kipling

You will feel on top of your game and will take events as they come seeing both the good and bad as part of a cycle of development. This year is all about your development regarding thinking more strategically, planning better, improving consistency, sticking to resolutions and aims and being tactical. 2017 is also about being observant and vigilant regarding keeping abreast of what you need to know to keep ahead in your workplace or in terms of family politics. This is a great year to use words wisely for conflict avoidance. Scorpio are known for rushing headlong into situations, but in 2017, you will be a little more artful in the way you approach delicate situations.

This is the year to solve problems with both determination and a little cunning – Scorpio will not let obstacles deter them, and you can be enormously resourceful in the way you approach hurdles, no matter how daunting. You will be amazed at your ability to problem solve and follow through; this can be exciting, and in many cases, you will feel vindicated when things start to turn your way.

You have the power to handle your emotions and channel all energy (both positive and negative) in a constructive way; this means stress will be less of a problem. What aids your concentration and also achievement levels is the greater balance between head and heart – your ego and spiritual will are lining up, and this lessening of inner conflict means you are not undermining yourself with negative subconscious motivations.

Everyday life has more significance and your work, your love life, and even somewhat innocuous events have importance and relevance. Often, little messages come to you via random comments or coincidences, and they often endorse what you are doing, feeling, or saying.

2017 is the time to get your message out. That message can be about your business and how you can help people via your services, or it could be a motivation or political/health related message you are trying to get out there to wake people up. Your own research or evidence gathering may help you uncover something important and little known.

Scorpio have good instincts this year; in general, Scorpio have a gut feel they can rely on, but this year, your intuition is enhanced as your mind is clear, and you can combine logic with emotional intelligence to make excellent decisions about long and short-term goals as well as personal issues.

Friends are significant to you in 2017, and you are often the to go to person for some TLC or mothering; you may act as a spiritual guide to those who are close to you or who become close during the year. New friendships with people beyond your usual social circle will be established due to a spiritual or emotional connection, i.e., you may connect with people who have gone through a similar experience. 2017 is a year when you will link up with groups for support regarding prenatal groups, postnatal support, weight loss groups, post-traumatic stress meetings, addiction groups, menopause support, LGBT issues, etc. – Scorpio are often loners, but this is not a year to 'suffer' alone or struggle alone; you can experience healing and also positivity via connecting with those at a similar stage of life. In a similar vein, Scorpio can be the catalyst for others to experience an epiphany regarding their own personal development.

In relationships, you are more sensitive, more in tune, and more willing to adapt to your partner's needs. You enjoy being caring and will see the things you do for your partner as a pleasure not a burden. Single Scorpio are ready to mingle and eager to meet an eclectic mix of new potential partners, but you will be slower to commit – it is a year where you are open to new relationships but want to take things at a slower and steady pace, not jumping right in. Scorpio's air of mystery will make them alluring and appealing and enhance their renowned sexual appeal. Scorpio are happy to embrace unusual romantic situations and will reserve judgement until they have really got to know the person – Scorpio will give lovers a fair chance, which is unusual as often Scorpio dismiss potential partners out of hand. In love, Scorpio will enjoy quality time with their partners, and this goes for new and established relationships, and so no hectic partying or socializing; more cozy times by the fire or long walks in the forest.

This year, Scorpio win when those around them win, and so it is not a selfish year – there is joy in being part of a team, a family or a movement where efforts are pooled and success shared.

There is both novelty and spontaneity in all your personal relationships, and this favours networking, team building, and work involving the public. Scorpio are very sensitive to the needs of their clients or customers and can react quickly to changing trends. It is a phenomenal year for organic growth, and hard work done throughout previous years will now start delivering dividends.

This is a year of thinking carefully about spending – if in doubt, hold back. It is an excellent time to plan pensions, set money aside or in the case of business conduct long-term investment. It is the year to spend money on serious tings rather than on frivolous ones – you may invest in yourself by buying a training course or invest in your home by making improvements or invest in your business. There can be investment in fixed assets with a view to long-term growth. Scorpio do have to take responsibility this year for past spending – so if you overspent over many years, this is one to pay down debt and cut back. However, this should not be seen as a bad thing; in fact, getting on top of your finances, being more hands on, less dependent on credit and building up savings will feel incredible good. This is a year of shoring up your financial base, making yourself more independent and beginning to feel more in control of your future financially.

This could be a year when you cut back radically in one area so that you can spend more in another, i.e., starting a business. It could also mean that you take a pay cut to become freelance or begin your own business – this will be a building year where you plough efforts into creating a strong base and platform. Scorpio will feel good about the way they are cutting back and saving, especially due the massive uncertainty in the world – it is your way of establishing security for yourself. Scorpio may invest in gold, silver, or other minerals rather than in stocks; you may also put your money into property to get a rental income.

Often, Scorpio forgo physical comforts to spend more money on what is emotionally satisfying or fulfils a dream – there can be a great amount of joy from the emotional and non-material side of life.

2017 is the year to finally kick bad habits for good. You tend to be more concerned with long-term impacts and less worried about short-term, impulsive satisfaction. So a wonderful time to become vegetarian, get into regular exercise, buy natural supplements to boost energy, kick out sugar, switch to organic. Many Scorpio may think about going off grid (getting more independent by using solar power), growing their own vegetables, cycling rather than using a gas guzzling car or taking their health and future into their own hands by radical lifestyle choices.

Everyday events and activities can trigger important changes in your life, and so nothing can be set aside as insignificant. Focus on details and keep your finger on the pulse. Scorpio will find it hard to delegate, and while micromanaging may take up your time, it may be a necessary evil. There are things which have become a part of your life, but which although you are not happy about them, you have put up with them to such an extent that you now accept them as the norm – now it is the time you will revisit these issues and scrap them ruthlessly.

Scorpio are ready to tackle difficult issues and to negotiate hard. You have no time for superficial dinner party chat; you are ready to broach difficult topics and get to grips with key issues. Scorpio will go to the heart of things not skirting around the issues; your approach can be quite hard hitting as you often take a controversial stand. The power is in your message, and if you have to shock to ram that message home, you will.

This can be a cathartic year, and that could be expressed via writing novels, autobiographies or self-help books – you can tap into and address your psychological issues via the medium of literature. This could also be a time when you read and write extensively on subjects like psychology, transformation, or personal struggle.

It is vital to own your thoughts and fears, or what you do not face can boomerang back to confront you. Do not allow subconscious anxieties and angers to control you; you may find that others pick up on your hidden aspects, and this can undermine your message. Achievement this year is closely linked to power of thought; harness the power of thoughts to shape your destiny and increase your effectiveness.

The more your outer actions mirror your internal emotional climate, the more powerfully you can influence others or be creative in your work – if you are a phony or a hypocrite, your house will come down like a pack of cards. If you cannot follow you heart regarding the direction you take in terms of research, publication, or management, you are likely to rebel.

Scorpio are in a transformative, reformist frame of mind; you are attracted to subjects beyond the mainstream and are driven to get at the truth and then inform others. It is an adventurous year on the mental plane with many concepts taking on a whole new meaning or relevance, and you engage in the world with vigour.

Established relationships are a rock, a safe space, and a source of strength. This is a good year for relationships – they may not be exciting or dramatic, but they will be solid, reliable, and comfortable. Commitment, loyalty, and the willingness of you both to work out problems and work at deepening understanding is emphasized in 2017. You are keen to help you partner and support him/her in their work and goals. You are a giver more than a taker in love this year.

New relationships are more romantic and experimental than the established ones but will progress at a slow pace. Scorpio are open to new love relationships, and potential lovers will be drawn to your gentle, mystical aura, but they will need to be patient, and you will not be rushed into commitment.

A year of revelations internally, of knowing yourself better, and of shaping your outer world to reflect your inner one. A time of joy from shared values and shared experiences, with new friendships that can enhance your life and show you new ways of thinking. A wonderful year for communicating and distributing ideas; you can become an intellectual leader or a trendsetting trail blazer in a world full of uncertainty. Scorpio are not sitting still; you are the people of tomorrow with your finger on the pulse.

This year is exciting on the mental plane, and you can be very influential. You can use words to help or inspire others and thoughts to reprogram your inner psychology and via that your outer reality.

LIFE

The year starts with a busy month that demands concentration and attention to detail. You need to be robust about how you put together your arguments or budgets – if you need to convince others, accuracy is essential. Clear and powerful facts backed up with figures help you nail home your argument.

Others may see you as erratic and unpredictable this month, but you are simply undergoing an internal shake-up where you are rejecting ideas and patterns of behaviour that are no longer helpful or reflective of who you are – those around you will have to get used to it.

Powerful platonic relationships with the opposite sex can be very enjoyable and also helpful to you as you shift gears this year both internally and externally.

Children can actually offer you advice, or the way they deal with adversity (your own children or those you teach) can teach you a few lessons.

Getting to grips with new technology for personal and professional use is a feature of this month. You may be able to find new avenues for self-expression via social media; although the warning is to get the feel of it slowly before you jump in wholeheartedly. If you have started a new blog, log or hang out online, be more patient about the results as you may be expected to take off like a rocket when in reality, it is a slow process of building and gaining ground.

LOVE

Relationships have to meet very high standards this year, and that is why although Scorpio are seeking out romantic relationship with potential lovers, they are not going to jump into something unless they are very sure. Sexual satisfaction is not the highest priority, love must be emotionally satisfying and rewarding on a spiritual level, and material considerations are well down the list. You are looking at people's souls and not at the labels the world has stamped on them, and in that way, it is a very non-judgemental time.

Scorpio may attract unwanted attention from someone who is very needy and who becomes emotionally attached or dependent on you wanting more than you can give – you need to manage this situation careful as it can escalate and become uncomfortable.

Children are important this month, and decisions about your children can bring you together as can sharing in their successes. It is an important time for family planning, which can include difficult decisions i.e., adoption, IVF treatment, etc., but the outcome is likely to be joyful.

This is a serious month in love; it is not about sex and spontaneity but rather about talking through problems, addressing key issues and solidifying your commitment. Scorpio who have been thinking about calling it quits on a bad relationship will probably use January as a clean break.

CAREER

Integrity is core to your success – you can demonstrate a commitment and belief in your ideas which are inspiring. Remember that what one set of people see as inspiring, others see as divisive; by having strong opinions, you are setting out on a difficult but rewarding route.

Scorpio have much guts and determination this month and are not deterred by doubters or seemingly impossible choices.

This is a very good month for those of you who research history or archaeology and whose work often consists of delving into the past and going through old records or archives. Scorpio who need to painstakingly analyze or sift through data will have their work rewarded.

Scorpio are excellent at spotting talent in people and seeing untapped potential – you can bring into the light the previously unseen or unappreciated.

This an a very rewarding month for Scorpio who work with children, especially if you are looking after their creative or emotional development – it will become apparent to you how closely the emotional and creative expression is linked, and you can help them build confidence. As I have said, they have as much to teach you as you do them.

This is a very productive and interesting month for those who work artistically with tools, i.e., jewellery making, sculpture, carpentry, crafting, and you may get exciting new equipment to work this.

A very good month for those who develop economic or mathematical models for prediction or analysis purposes.

An excellent month for anyone starting a new job.

LIFE

This is the month you may begin to renovate or add value to your home by modernising. Moves that happen now will go smoothly and will signify a new start for you. Home moves that happen now will be for the purpose of greater security, greater convenience and comfort, i.e., you may move somewhere where there is less traffic or less noise and more privacy, or you may build walls or plant trees to make your home more pleasant.

It is also a time when there are many family activities, and the focus may be on important events to do with family members, i.e., weddings, retirement parties, christenings, etc.

The home is an important centre of activity, and you will also take on a mothering role (regardless of whether you are female of not) to extended family members. You may cater for family events or offer up spare rooms or sofas for visiting family members. You are a person who is in demand right now; if you are older, you will be the matriarch of the family; if you are younger, you may be called upon to act like an older sister to siblings or cousins.

Emotional needs are stronger and more urgent; it will become apparent who supports you and nurtures you and who is just a drain – you will be generous with your affection and your time, but after this month you will have a much clearer idea about who deserves your care and who abuses it.

This is a strong month for parental instincts, and if you do not have children, you will be broody. You may suffer from empty nest syndrome, but this may be the impetus to be more involved with nieces and nephews. You will tend to be more worried and protective over your children, and this could signify a time when your children are growing up and becoming less dependent, and this can cause an identity crisis where you feel less needed. Many may decide to return to work as the children are now at school.

It is hard to see things in perspective this month, but things are actually better than you think. You have a quiet confidence and optimism right now, and while at times you may question that confidence in light of logic or developments, you just cannot shift the feeling that things are indeed working out for good.

This month can often see Scorpio returning to a strong faith based approach to life – it is a satisfying month for those who are religious or who have an open-minded attitude to life and the universe. You can see your life is part of a divine plan, and it feels good.

LOVE

A very good month for Valentine's Day and love. You should plan your Valentine's Day ahead of time, as when it comes you may feel a little lazy, and it would be a lost opportunity to do something special and memorable. Ideal plans are weekends away, somewhere secluded rather than a hectic trip like going to Vegas.

Single Scorpio should accept invitations to Valentine's Day parties or events as this is a good month to meet like-minded people with whom you can have a meaningful connection. This is a very good time to make a good impression. Your romantic instincts are good now, and you will sense subtle nuances allowing you to make the right move.

In long-term relationships, you should not take things for granted just because you are both relaxed and easygoing – use this time to make plans for the year ahead and also to make romance orientated plans. Relationships can go into decline when you stop doing fun things together, and so what better month to think about the things you used to enjoy together and reintroduce them.

In general, all relationships are warm and friendly, and this can be the start of a new chapter if things have been strained. The only negative is that you may not make the most of the opportunities for starting new relationships or improving existing ones; you may just think it is a good time for a breather rather than reform.

Scorpio need to be more cognisant of toying with the feelings of others – make sure they know where they stand regarding where you see it going. Relationships that begin now may remain in the friendship phase for a longer period than the other person is expecting.

CAREER

Often, career goals have to be subordinated to your family concerns, and you may even take time off work to move or devote time to family.

February is a very good month for starting a business in real estate, interior design or catering. It is very favourable for family businesses, especially those that are connected to construction or hospitality.

Work-life balance and priority considerations are vital this month. This could be the month where you change to a more flexible type of employment which can give you more freedom to pursue important family goals without neglecting those you love for the sake of work. Family events may force your hand regarding what your priorities are. In some cases, the opposite is true where you are now able to devote more time to work goals due to family commitments lessening.

This is a month of careful consideration rather than a surge forward – you will take time to review the options and delay decisions until it feels right.

Many things which happen now are directly related to past events – this can serve as a guide. The past is not always a good predictor of the future, but this month, the past is a very reliable barometer – if someone let you down or was a bad partner before, then write them off, no second chances as they are unlikely to be any better the second time around.

This is a very good month for settling legal matters, foreign investments, and international trade.

Small scale work related to social events can help foster camaraderie and team building.

LIFE

Self-expression this month is vital, and that makes this an important time for personal goals and engaging in activities that fulfil you and allow you to be yourself and take centre stage.

There is a desire to engage in new sports or creative activities to broaden out your life and increase contact with others and discover parts of yourself that have long been suppressed or hidden. This is an excellent time for those who have felt inhibited or held back as suddenly you feel more assertive and confident. You can act in ways that are true to yourself, and you may get the chance within your work to explore your ideas and take more control of projects so that you can put your personal stamp on them. This is definitely the start of making your mark on the world.

This is a month of pleasure, and you are likely to attend events, social occasions or grand openings. You will want to have a good time and feel young again. In many cases, you will enjoy these events with your children. You may travel to new places for short holidays; it is likely you will visit places like Disneyland, Vegas, Dubai, or other pleasure playgrounds with a huge variety of activities to offer.

LOVE

Romantic relationships that foster your own self-development and encourage a flowering of your personality will do very well; while relationships where you feel stifled or restrained by your partner will suffer, and you will feel the need to rebel.

New relationships can play a key role in building your confidence and expanding your horizons. The sexual side of relationships becomes more important as you feel increasingly physically attracted to your new partner. New relationships will bring out the best in you, and even if you have suffered from self-esteem issues, you can become more self-assured, and that includes sexually.

I did say that sex life is not key to this year; it is, however, key to this month when your sexual desires are powerful. You tend to be passionate and dramatic in love and even arguments are rather beneficial as they can clear the air and even pave the way to some excellent sex.

Emotions run high this month, and interaction can be intense – which is why you need to alternate time together with time when you go your separate ways to have a little breather. While you crave the stability, it is actually the dynamic nature of your relationship which brings more satisfaction.

CAREER

Scorpio are ready to take the limelight, and this month is an excellent time for all performers and artists who are launching projects or promoting themselves. This favours creative pursuits and also those creative projects which rely heavily on technology, i.e., graphic design, music production, film editing, etc.

Development of ideas is a key part of this month; not all ideas have to be creative in nature, they can be in terms of business plans, marketing strategies, investment options – whatever they are you need to flush them out this month and get them ready to take to the next level.

Scorpio are happy to task risks artistically – you will take some gambles and see if you can pull it off and make it work. Scorpio have a daredevil attitude, and you will back yourself to pull off more daring challenges at work and personally. You have a nothing to lose attitude and win or lose, you will gain by the experience.

Work with children is very rewarding, and great progress can be made. This month is great for teachers, paediatricians, social workers, and any person who works with children as you can establish a rapport which will aid you in understanding the child/children and addressing their problems or issues with sensitivity and effectiveness.

A great month for Scorpio seeking patents for inventions and also for branding of your products, trade name or indeed yourself as a personality.

LIFE

This month can be one that is filled with annoyances and irritations when it comes to other people. You may rub people up the wrong way with your opinions and visa versa – so I suggest staying away from Twitter or Facebook discussions where you will end up arguing and wasting your own time. This is a month when it is not easy to change the minds of others, no matter how hard you try. In some cases, it is best not to bother, but if there is much at stake and you feel you must try and influence someone (like a child or colleague), then you need to change your approach – do not act in a confrontational way, try and bring them around to your way of thinking slowly.

This is a very active time mentally, and you can get much work done, although the mantra is more haste less speed as you will tend to rush things as you are impatient. So take a little more time as details matter. Cultivate more self-discipline, and make sure you finish one thing before jumping to the next.

In physical situations, there is a tendency to over-extend yourself, so make sure that you do stay within your limits and build up slowly rather than hitting the ground running.

Care should be take when travelling, and this is not a good time to risk being on the phone while driving as you could get a fine.

There is a high degree of energy available to you this month, and while this can be used to make progress, initiate action and tackle problems successfully, it can also lead to confrontations and stress – so to harness the positive, you have to focus on anger constructively and pick your battles carefully, avoiding no-win arguments and conflicts. Know when to walk away.

LOVE

It is very important not to make assumptions about your partner or your relationship and then act on those as if they are factual. You can get so convinced that your view is correct that you forget to have a discussion and talk it through, and you go right on acting according to these assumptions rather than to reality. This can be very confusing and frustrating to your partner, as in a way they are not getting the right of reply – you are acting as judge, jury, and prosecutor without a key witness.

So, before you jump to conclusions, get all the information you need and allow your partner a right of reply and hear him/her out. Air grievances, but do concentrate on central issues rather than letting tempers flare over peripheral issues.

This is a very good time for rebalancing relationships – if you feel that you are either not appreciated, listened to or respected, this is your time to put your foot down and say, "Hey, what about me!" It is also a good time to get things back to 50:50 regarding work put into the relationship – it's a two-way street, not a one-way highway.

Forgiveness on your part can ensure that progress is made and you do not get stuck in an unproductive stalemate; nothing can be gained from stubbornness right now, and so set grievances aside and move on. Things can work out, but you have to be the bigger person and take the lead.

This is a very good month for couples who work together and who have big goals set for this year.

CAREER

While teamwork can be frustrating, it can also be very productive – it could be down to how you handle your temper or irritation. You have the power to lead or be a disruptive influence on the group – however, you can probably achieve more by taking up the reigns and leading by showing the way and working hard rather than throwing the toys out of the trolley and walking away.

Scorpio who have been experiencing a writer's block in terms of finding that your creative juices have stopped flowing will discover that the muse returns during mid-month, and once again you can generate great ideas and get your projects moving.

There are some conflicts of interests regarding finances this month, and you may delay investment decisions until you have a better idea of what your key goals are this year. You may feel pulled in one direction; however, you may realise that logically another route is more likely to succeed, and this head-heart battle can hold you back from making firm decisions.

Scorpio may experience delays in getting paid bonuses or commission due to mistakes in administration, and you will have to chase these up.

This is a very successful month for businesses which cater to children, i.e., toys, games, school accessories or clothing. Indeed, all businesses, i.e., restaurants, hotels, B&Bs, etc., should look to be more kiddie or baby friendly.

All Scorpio in communication industries need to knuckle down and focus on your work as you can achieve a great deal in April as long as you set targets and have clear goals. It is vital to look below the surface and to follow every lead through – this is a month when you can get caught out by slimming the surface. Always prepare 50% more than you will need, and you are prepared for anything. An excellent time for investigative journalism.

LIFE

You can be extremely persuasive this month – unlike last month, you are better at tapping into the mood music and playing to it. Scorpio are known for being manipulative, and although that may seem a negative work, it can be a key life skill, and you will be using it this month especially in business and competitive situations.

It is a very good month for mass communications – that means communicating with people way beyond your social or work circle to reach people you have never even met – your YouTube video or Facebook post may go viral. It is a time when you can gain attention by being controversial. Scorpio may use this month to push important issues often ignored, i.e., homelessness, social decay or corruption.

Your many interesting ideas will attract new friends and also colleagues who will want to work with you. Scorpio may come into possession of secret information this month, and you could sit on it a while waiting to decide what to do, i.e., you may discover a colleague being dishonest, financial irregularities, or even that a friend's partner is cheating. Deciding what to do can be hard as there are many complications and factors to consider. As long as you think it through, you will make a just decision. You should keep your own counsel – beware of talking about this situation to others who are involved.

LOVE

This month is best for couples who work together, i.e., in a small business or in the same type of job. You will have much to discuss about your work and developments in your industry, and this fosters good communication and can bring you together, despite any other differences.

Like the above paragraph, this is also a very good month for new relationships which begin in offices or workplaces. Scorpio are excited about and immersed in their work this month, and so it flows that the more your partner understands your work and supports you in it or even shares that interest, the better the relationship will go. New romances will start with a solid base of shared values and interests as reflected in the line of work you have chosen.

This is a more challenging month for Scorpio who have partners who are very different, i.e., the opposites attract syndrome. In these relationships, fostering understanding takes quite a bit of energy and compromise as the differences can seem greater than that which binds you this month.

Arguments are likely about the joint bank account and where to spend and where to save – you will both fight for what you want, and it can get heated.

Sexually, this month can be very exciting, but the sex is not necessarily spontaneous – it is more about planning the time, getting the kids babysitters, and setting up a conducive space for romance and sex to flourish. Sex needs forethought, and it also needs some delicacy regarding expressing what you need and what you would prefer. You need to relax before sex as you are both very tense, and this can affect performance – so take your time to get into the groove with food, wine, music, etc.

CAREER

This month is one where Scorpio who work as war correspondents, press officers for defence ministries, the military or aerospace industries can come into the limelight. It is a very important month for all of you who work in communication to report with great integrity as what you print or publish can have wide ramifications.

This is also a very exciting time for Scorpio who are travelling to conventions to go with green energy, science, or archaeology – you may travel to report on or further investigate a new discovery.

Scorpio who work in any forensic capacity from medicine to accounting can have very interesting work and possibly the chance to testify or write important reports.

This is also an important month for work on pathology, i.e., development of vaccines, antidotes, and natural therapies.

This month is a superb one for Scorpio studying psychology or anthropology (and completing papers) or who are practising. Your insights into the human condition and fundamental causes of depression or mental issues can be quite remarkable, and you could become very well known in your sphere.

Travel for work this month could mean travel to places which are dangerous, crime-ridden, or in decay – this can be a fascinating or enlightening experience. Your trips this month (even if short) will not be mundane; they will contain vital gems of information that can inform your work or stimulate your imagination.

LIFE

Things are going well this month although you may not appreciate this as some of the positive events are subtle and could even escape your notice or happen without your awareness. Someone may pay you a good deed behind your back, which results in an unexpected benefit.

This can be a very good month regarding your goals as you are not so ego driven that you cannot see yourself in perspective and acknowledge your mistakes; you will be able to see where you have been wrong, and you will correct that even if it means putting your pride in your pocket. Often this month, two steps back is the best way to make four steps forward.

This month, you can forge alliances with people who you are usually opposed to regarding values, aims or beliefs as suddenly you are in the same boat and have a common goal or enemy – this can be very exciting and can give you a brand new perspective on people who you were previously at odds with.

This is a pleasant and sociable month where you are easygoing and can find time for pleasure and relaxation. Overindulgence is a problem, and you will not be able to resist sugary and fatty foods, and so not a good month for diets.

This is an inspirational month for those for whom faith plays an important role in life – you may get more involved in church/mosque/temple related activities, especially when it comes to reaching out to other religious groups, building bridges, and increasing understanding. You may also get involved in charity connected to the church.

You have a strong inner faith that defies logic and reason but which is palpable – it is probably better to keep this to yourself as others will most certainly pour cold water on your feelings, telling you it's not rational.

LOVE

This is a great month for love. You are affectionate, loving, and giving, and will promote bonhomie in all relationships. New relationships will be fun and carefree, and neither of you will want to ruin the mood with any heavy conversations or serious talks about where the relationship is going. It is all about fun and enjoyment and escapism through love.

The only problem for love is that Scorpio are less patient with partners who are maudlin – you will be likely to shift your focus to friends rather than be with a sulky or troubled boyfriend or husband.

Scorpio want to enjoy the month and will expect their partners to snap out of moods or miserable attitudes.

Scorpio are very amorous this month which bodes well for existing relationships; however, single Scorpio may be so caught up in the moment and the good vibe that they take things too far regarding flirting or being indiscreet. This can lead to awkward moments in the coming months, and so do not get carried away.

This month, Scorpio are very romantic, and they will express this by writing poetry, songs, or even preparing special meals to show their love. Scorpio want to share and do things with their loved one – like the song "It takes two." – Everything is sweeter for Scorpio when they share it with a romantic partner.

CAREER

This month can be a frustrating one for those who work in public service; you may have to do extra work for less pay, or your pay rise may not be a real increase. This month will test your motivations; if you work in nursing or policing or any other sphere of government you will need to work for the love of the job or the belief in what you are doing – if you are there for the sake of money, power, or ambition, it is likely to be a disappointing time. However, if you love the work for the value you create for others, this will be a rewarding month. Selfless service is hugely rewarding as the spoils this month are appreciation from those whose lives you touch rather than from the boss or the pay cheque. Scorpio who are motivated by public service will find added energy and compassion this month, and you can make a big difference to those you serve.

This is a very good month for those training in the medical arena, i.e., trainee nurses, doctors, physiotherapists and occupational therapists. Many Scorpio may quit jobs in business or admin to take on a more service orientated career that is more hands on and which utilises your compassionate nature.

June is very good for all creative and artistic work, especially where you are collaborating with other artists. This is a very good time to form a band, start an art group, start a theatre or dance company. If you work in the arts and are recruiting or looking for funding for a tour, this is a great month. It is a good month for starting tours and mounting promotional campaigns.

Those whose work is very seasonal and relies on the summer months for most of their trade will see strong demand this month, and it will bode well for the next three months.

LIFE

This month is one of creative change where you will have the inner resolve and also the tenacity to reform circumstances in your daily life that have become troublesome, time wasting, or intolerable. Often, you have had to put up with something for some time, and now it's the month when you will put your foot down and say, "No more!"

This is a month when you need to seize the opportunities for taking power that come your way – these can come via your job or in your personal life. The more you strive to improve yourself and your day to day life, the more success you will have as the energy is there to be used for this purpose. This month is thus also good for taking control of daily habits to do with food and exercise.

This is a good time to get more organised: clear out your basement, reorganise your office or change your computerised systems to save you time. Scorpio need to feel more in control of their daily lives, and that means making sure your family contributes to chores and you all carry your weight; it also means re-thinking the way you travel to work to save time or money or ensuring colleagues do not freeload. This is also a time when small changes like a chair that is better for your back, a quieter work space or a new piece of equipment can make a very big difference to your day.

This is a good time for taking on tasks where thorough and detailed work is required and where concrete, measurable results can be achieved.

Your persuasive powers are strong, and you are thus able to negotiate and sell your ideas or products with zeal.

This is an exciting month for Scorpio in higher education, and you may be involved in student committees and leadership positions – you may strive to get student issues high on the political agenda.

LOVE

Scorpio are loved for their passion, depth of feeling, and exciting energy, and this is on full display this month. Scorpio are at their intense magnetic best, and this will stimulate both the communication and sexual side of new and established relationships. You have much to give to the union and you can inject a spark which may have been lacking for a while.

Single Scorpio will have no shortage of admirers; however, will they satisfy you? That is the question. Scorpio are quite insatiable emotionally, and so they may cultivate many different love relationships in different areas, i.e., at work, online or via your usual social circles. There is this tendency to keep more than one potential lover on the go, and while that can work for a while, it can get very complicated when some or all of them want to get serious, and so bear that in mind.

This is once again a very sexual month, and Scorpio may exhaust their partner. Problems in your sex life will be highlighted and will demand attention – but this can be a very good thing for the future of your sex life and so do not shy aware from the intimate conversations.

This can be a very tricky month for divorces regarding legalities and also in terms of one or both of you being difficult due to lingering hurt feelings – remember that often the cleaner the break, the better for both of you, and so know when to bury the hatchet and stop playing games.

Ex-partners suddenly pitching up can disrupt new relationships or cause you to have mixed feelings; remember the only way is forward NOT back, and so remember why the previous relationship went wrong and do not expect a different result a second time.

CAREER

This month you need to review your PC systems – how effective are they; how safe are they; how cost effective are they? You may need to overhaul your website to make it more user-friendly or less prone to attack or hacking. It is very important to protect against malware and ransomware.

Last month was about the emotional and spiritual rewards of work; this month is more about the concrete ones.

This is an excellent month for Scorpio who work in careers which involve problem-solving, i.e., detectives, researchers, product developers or those dealing with complex legal issues and fine print. There is a great desire to solve these problems and a large amount of perspective on how to tackle things in the best way. There is a strong desire to look below the surface and look far deeper than the immediate issues. Scorpio in business can make very perceptive decisions now as you will look at a wider range of data and factors than your competitors and will thus be better tuned in to the market.

If you work in trade this month, it is vital to improve logistics, speed up delivery times or improve customer service.

This is a good month to plan business related travel, especially if it is to do with managing staff in overseas branches or in a business management training role. It is also a great month for travelling if you are in sports and are travelling to compete.

LIFE

This month, Scorpio may look to move house, relocate and rent out your house or even do a house swap as you spend an extended period away from home.

Home moves this month tend to be to a different town or environment, i.e., town to city or vice versa and can involve some adjustment of even learning a new language. This can be a disruptive time but also a chance to make a fresh start.

This is certainly a month to move on emotionally even if not physically from situations that have held you back. It is time to kick negative habits, i.e., holding on to anger, being resentful and even being over sentimental. You should not romanticise the past; it does not matter how good or bad the past was – it is finished, and the future is all you have, and so do not let regrets, pain, or longing for the past cast a shadow over what you should be striving for now.

While you should forgive yourself and others for events in the past, you should not necessarily forget as patterns tend to repeat, and so you do need to take the past behaviour of a person as a good indicator of their expected future behaviour.

Talking about patterns, there will be many events this month which strongly echo events which have happened before; this can thus be a fabulous opportunity to do things differently this time and thus break a cycle and even release yourself mentally from a block which had developed.

This is certainly a month to get back on the horse – do not be deterred by failure, get right back into it and try again. The only way you fail is if you give up.

In August, you are best going it alone regarding goals as friends can be a distraction; let them do their thing, and you do yours, and do not count on their support.

LOVE

This is a month when love affairs with friends can be tricky. If you have a friend who became a lover or romantic partner, now could be the month when you want to switch their status back to friend and that can be a problem as they may not want to accept that. It is best not to form romances with friends this month if it has not already happened. Be sure that there are no mixed messages between you and platonic friends.

This is a withdrawal phase where Scorpio will become non-committal in relationships – it is almost as if you are getting cold feet and you need privacy and a chance to think things through. I can see Scorpio not answering phones and emails, just to get a mental and emotional breather.

This is certainly not the month where Scorpio will want to formalise a commitment by getting married, moving in or going steady (if that is still the done thing) – so if you are going out with a Scorpio, do not plan a proposal or elopement this month.

In long-term relationships, Scorpio may come across as withdrawn and may need more space. There is much happening for Scorpio at a deep internal level right now, and they need time to think, ponder, and reassess. They will not tolerate nagging and pressure. This can often seem like a negative phase in the relationship, but it is not negative as much as a chance for pause and reflection before heading forward. However, in relationships that have been going badly, this is a time of drifting further apart – not arguing, just a fading of feeling and intensity.

The best relationships this month are long distance, alternative and age gap relationships. Open relationships also thrive.

CAREER

This month is a tough one creatively as you will face doubts and opposition from others; you may even fail to get approval or acknowledgment from your teacher or mentor. It is hard to learn from your mistakes as sometimes you will have to make changes to elements of your work which are of deep personal significance. This is certainly a hard month for artistic work that is deeply emotionally inspired as when there is so much of you in your work, making changes and dealing with rejection is that much harder. It is also a hard month to get your ideas accepted by peers and associates, and you will need a thick skin. Remember that while some criticism is helpful, not all of it is worth listening to, and you have to be very selective about what kind of criticism you are exposing yourself to. Develop a thick skin (which I know is hard for Scorpio, you prefer to plot your revenge, which is best served cold of course), and remember that success is often the best form of revenge, so do not give up.

There is a great deal of uncertainty this month regarding global markets and stocks, as well as global politics, and Scorpio are feeling this keenly. You do feel uncertain of how to proceed, and it is best not to make significant investments or new contracts this month.

This is not a good month to start a new business, launch a product or start a major new campaign. Sit tight, hold back, and wait and see.

Your confidence is not very high this month – which is quite OK; it is normal and part of a natural phase of internal questioning and development. This month is best for the private and non-public nurturing of your ideas, projects, or business and is not a good time for public roles or going for promotion. You are not best placed to launch forward; this is a consolidation period.

Press relations and media work need to be undertaken with a great deal of caution – check facts carefully. Long-term plans will suffer short-term problems, and you will have to make some very fast adjustments which will test your ability to make the right decision in a hurry.

LIFE

The emphasis is back on career, reputation, and your role in the outer world this month. This is a better month for pushing ahead and working on your goals, and you will have a far better idea about what to do and how to do it.

Younger Scorpio may find that their parents are influencing their career decisions this month and this can be welcome, i.e., when they help you get a job via their connections or insider knowledge or a hindrance where they expect you to follow in their career footsteps. Either way, parents will play a role in your life direction as they will help you or actually force you to rebel and follow a new direction which can be very successful.

There is a stage Mother syndrome this month where some parents expect you to live out their dream and are overbearing in their attempts to steer you – this will force you to set some boundaries and learn where the parent ends and you begin, and this can be a watershed time for you.

LOVE

This is a good month for love relationships of all sorts. One of the problems is that you may both get caught in an upward or downward spiral. If you are caught in the upward spiral, this can mean you both behave rather hedonistically by fuelling each other's emotions or passions, and this may lead to your overspending or indulging in general. If it is a downward spiral, you may plummet into negativity or anger – it is important for you both to act as a brake for the other, not an accelerator.

It is important for Scorpio to look at any childhood conditioning that may be affecting relationships. Often the way we experience our parents' relationship casts a long shadow. If we saw our parents have a great marriage, we assume that this is achievable and act accordingly, but if we had a parent who was single and perhaps rejected, we may fear rejection and almost expect it, and that can lead to a self-fulfilling prophesy. If we saw a parent put up with abuse, we may also be too self-sacrificing in relationships, the people pleaser, the perpetual forgiver. It is very important for Scorpio to write their own script regarding relationships – you are not your parents, and there is no need for you to follow in their path. It can often be hard to spot this happening as much of it will take place on a subconscious level, but you need to be alert to behaviours that are learned rather than ones which are appropriate.

Make sure you start new relationships with a clean slate and do not allow yourself to self-sabotage existing relationships based on notions about relationships passed on from your parents.

CAREER

September is the month to pick up the forward momentum again. You can make some decisions, and you will feel you have a better grip on all the factors at stake.

Recognition begins to come your way, and this is a far better time for publicity and self-promotion. Hard work and diligence will now be rewarded, and the extra effort you have put in will stand you in good stead. If, however, you have cut corners, the light could be shone on your failings, and so make sure of your remedy and shore up your work before putting it out there. Remember that your reputation is at stake now, and so be careful of having a consistent image and message and watch out what you commit to Twitter and social media. The past will catch up with you this month, so either reward or trouble is on the way, depending on how you have acted. If you know this in advance, you can make sure you have acted appropriately in the run-up.

Those who are self-employed can be very successful this month based on the strength of your personality and your ability to be in touch with the public and satisfy their needs. Those who are very hands-on in the business can react faster to changes in customer needs or trends, and this leads to success and good performances.

Learning and mastering professional techniques or joining professional organisations is important this month. If you can take extra professional qualifications and get more letters after your name, this can enhance your credibility and the chance of moving ahead.

As leader, you need to motivate and enthuse those you employ or those you manage; you cannot lead by authority alone, it is about leading by example. If you are an employee, you need to show initiative and the ability to carry out instructions but also to use your own judgement.

LIFE

This month marks Jupiter's entry in Scorpio and the start of a 12-year period of expansion and personal growth and opportunity. It is time to recognise your need for new pastures and also a degree of adventure in your life. This is the beginning of a year where you will feel more pioneering and pro-active. The degree of success and property (both material and spiritual) this year is in direct proportion to what you believe you deserve, and so it is important to develop self-esteem and to be in touch with your needs to get the most out of this time. You need to halt patterns of self-denial, brutal self-criticism and a feeling of being undeserving. You need to embrace the mantras of 'I CAN' and 'I deserve the very best in life' and keep saying them to yourself.

Reach out and feel the power in the universe. Let it flow through you and allow the light to shine into your soul, banishing dark and destructive thoughts.

The more you value yourself and your attributes, the greater confidence you will have; there is nothing to be gained now from being self-effacing – this is where a confident and positive new you emerges. You have much to offer others this coming year regarding guidance and wisdom, but you also have much to offer yourself – you must embrace new opportunities and not be held back. You should be at the top of your list right now as this period will bring opportunities that can shape the next decade of your life and are thus not to be missed.

Test yourself by taking on challenges and trying things which push your boundaries – it is time to extend your beliefs about what is or is not possible.

The power for creative change and widening horizons is there, but it cannot happen without you reaching out to tap into that energy and getting the ball rolling – so this cannot be a passive 'wait for a lotto win' time; it must be an active period of planning and implementation of potential life-changing or defining goals.

LOVE

Love life can be disrupted this month. Your partner may have to go away for work or perhaps it is you who will have to go away, and there will be a period spent apart – however, this can be a very good thing. You need space in relationships right now; this is not really a cosy month where you want to live in each other's pocket.

While much of this year you were happy to spend time with your partner, often alone and enjoying a relaxed togetherness, you are clicking into a different phase where you are far more restless and need to either go off on your own and experience new things or do exciting things with your partner. You will be the one to initiate changes which will make your marriage or partnership more spontaneous and inject some novelty in day to day life and sex life.

New relationships can start suddenly and develop along unusual lines, but this will be perfect for you right now as you are looking for unconventional relationships that have excitement and which do not tie you down.

In establishment relationships, Scorpio will set new ground rules, and those will most certainly involve more freedom for you!

CAREER

Many of your plans may be kept close to your chest this month. In a way, you need to cultivate and develop them before anyone has the chance to pour cold water on them.

The biggest problem this month is that you are not very practical – you are great in terms of brainstorming, having vision, foresight, and seeing the bigger picture, but you may fall down when it comes to detail and actual practicalities. You can benefit from working with people who do have the more practical or administrative skills.

It is also important to be pragmatic – sometimes it's good to have high ideals and espouse great moral concepts, but to get things done you often need to be a realist, and that can mean making a deal with the Devil. In other words, you may have to get along with people who you really do not like for the sake of business or form temporary contracts with people in your industry whom you do not approve of for many reasons. This can be a good learning experience, even though it will try your patience and you will have to bite your tongue. The lesson is that in life you do not always get to work with people you like, but these relationships can work and be productive for you.

Aggressive pursuit of goals is not the best way to go about achieving them; patience is paramount and so is timing. Things cannot be hurried along, and so be constant and persevering.

Pacing yourself is vital as your energy will be drained by working with these people you usually avoid, but at the same time, your energy can surge as this is also a very inspirational time.

LIFE

This month, you may have to clean up a mess that was not of your making. It can be that you take over a position in which another person has set things in motion, and now you are lumbered with the consequences, or you may feel obliged to help someone else out with problems as you feel responsible for that person.

November is a month of labours of love – a time when you are happy to put in extra effort or even conduct laborious thankless work because something matters to you on a higher level. Material values are less important and spiritual matters perhaps disguised as creative, or humanitarian pursuits will take precedence.

Often Scorpio experience the divine via hobbies and interests which you follow, and even if you are not religious, you will have a greater sense of the interconnectivity of life and the special meaning behind events. ESP and psychic feelings are stronger, and you may also have a strong sense of family members who have died – you may feel their presence more than usual or see them in dream in a positive and supportive way.

This is a very idealistic time in your life when you are thinking big and have a much more broad-minded and tolerant approach to people and concepts. You can be rather dreamy and distracted in November as your internal life is extremely rich, and you will tend to drift off into an exciting world of imagination. Visualisation techniques can be used right now to great effect, and it is also a good time for envisioning your future and getting a clear mental picture of what your goals look like.

LOVE

This is a romantic month and also one where fantasy plays an important role.

Love and romance cannot be mundane or ordinary as you need far more than that. Scorpio are keen to experiment, to play out some fantasies and to be more open with their partner. It is a time when Scorpio are looking to take intimacy to a new level in both established and newer relationships. Superficial actions and words are not enough to keep the fires of love fuelled – there must be intensity, honest, openness, and a revival of the spiritual connection.

Relationships where you have both drifted in different directions regarding hopes and dreams will suffer. Scorpio are entering a very idealistic and also a questioning phase in life where deeper meaning and significance is sought. So where Scorpio is with someone who is very materialistic or concerned with the mundane, romance can falter. Of course, Scorpio value stability and security, and so if the partner is a good anchor, things can still rattle along, as long as the Scorpio has friends or other family with whom to share their visions, dreams, and interesting new avenues of thought.

However, Scorpio love to be on the same page as their life partner, and so where you have gone separate ways regarding your view of the world and / or of life, things can be difficult, especially as the Scorpio will try their best to bring the partner around to their way of thinking.

In relationships where you are naturally inclined to dynamic ways of thinking, embracing new concepts, spirituality, and alternative thinking, this will be a great month. Shared dreams equal passion in the bedroom; so partners of Scorpio need to get with the script.

CAREER

Scorpio are good leaders but reluctant leaders as leadership often involves a loss of privacy and a loss of control, but this month you may have leadership thrust upon you just because you are the most knowledgeable on a subject or best prepared, not because you necessarily want the position. This chance to take up the reigns can have a few effects: you can learn more about your ability to manage and lead, and you can get a valuable experience for the resume.

This is a time of balance where you can implement the new while still maintaining structure – there are less tricky compromises to be made, and you can effectively have your cake and eat it as well.

Changes that begin as challenges quickly become part of your everyday life, and your ability to adapt and master new technical or scientific methods is excellent.

While the need for change and new opportunities is strong, you have the patience needed to wait for the right time and sense where the best opportunities lie. You can set out your plans in a logical and yet original way, and this will gain you the support you need.

What Scorpio are masters of right now is having the right blend of originality and yet also that ability to work within existing structures and guidelines. Your ideas are exciting but not outlandish or threatening, and this is why you will get acceptance for your ideas as well as funding or the green light.

You can impress your superiors or your lecturers right now with the quality of your work and the systematic and thorough way in which you set out your stall.

No matter what came before you (in terms of you taking over a position from someone else), you can take the best of what they were doing forward while knowing how to radically alter what they were not doing very well.

LIFE

This is an excellent December for Scorpio. You will be relaxed, happy and benevolent, and there will be good times spent with quality friends and your favourite family members.

This is a good month for health, and your powers of recuperation are strong. If you have been working very hard, this is a great month to let your hair down and have fun.

The only bad side of this month is that you are prone to extravagance and over-indulgence, and this can undo some of the very good work you did this year to pay off debt and get good health regimes into place. I know you feel pretty invincible right now, but take care and don't overdo it.

Scorpio will enjoy their seasonal shopping enjoying buying gifts and spoiling others close to you. Scorpio will use this season more so than usual to build bridges and thank people who you feel have supported and blessed you this year.

You should enjoy some excellent social events in December which include dining out, trips away to shop in different locales or reunions with old colleagues.

Although some hard work still has to be done, the vibe this month is happy and positive, and you will achieve quite a bit effortlessly due to your good mood.

LOVE

Scorpio are more realistic and feet on the ground regarding love this month, and while you are still after intensity and creative change in the marriage, you are also more practical about the way that has to happen.

Scorpio are giving their partners some leeway – you know they may be tired and overworked, and you are happy to make allowances.

Relationships tend to work well this month, and you can come together effectively regarding making this a wonderful Christmas for your children and your wider family – there is a highly cooperative spirit. You are more than willing to meet your partner's needs, and they will meet yours.

Scorpio in new relationships are less starry eyed and more realistic about the prospects and pitfalls of their new love match – this is a great thing as you will see where more work needs to be done and what the relationship can offer you. New relationships have much to teach you, and you are very eager to learn; that means you are more willing to stay in relationships that have challenges as you know those challenges are the gateways to a better and more rounded you.

2017 ends on a very good note for your relationships – this has been a revealing year regarding your love life, and you have learned much about yourself.

CAREER

It is wise to be careful with cash flow this month – do not count on money until it clears into your account. Mercury retrograde can cause delays in payments, banking glitches or invoicing problems, and so watch those areas. Make sure you have plenty of cash in hand, just in case due to weather or a banking problem cash machines are closed in the run-up to the holidays. Pay bills a few days earlier as websites being down may make paying them on the due day impossible.

Clients may be slower to pay, which can have a knock-on effect on your business, and so this is not a good month for incurring unnecessary expenses.

Scorpio will have to do a strong push during December to make sure they reach targets needed to ensure bonus payments – do not take anything for granted, follow up on all your clients, and get those orders in.

This is a very busy month for those who work in accounts, admin, and finance – it can be quite an unpredictable time, and you may have to work extra hard to keep on top of events.

This month, your work socials or your customer seasonal events will be very pleasant and successful and should proceed without the usual stress. December is also very good for running promotions and customer incentives – these can increase sales.

Those who work in hairdressing, nail technicians, the beauty industry or fashion can have a very successful December. This month is also very profitable for those who manage or promote the arts, i.e., concert sales, theatre bookings, and other entertainment events.

This is a very good year end career-wise for Scorpio, and you will look forward to 2018 with confidence.

THANK YOU SO MUCH FOR BUYING MY BOOK AND SUPPORTING ME. GOD BLESS AND ALL THE BEST FOR 2017 AND 2018.

Made in the USA
Lexington, KY
21 December 2016